SURRENDERING TO GOD

POETRY TO ENCOURAGE A CLOSER WALK WITH CHRIST

RYAN DILLMAN

WestBow Press
A DIVISION OF THOMAS NELSON & ZONDERVAN

Copyright © 2023 Ryan Dillman.

All rights reserved. No part of this book may be used or reproduced by any means, graphic, electronic, or mechanical, including photocopying, recording, taping or by any information storage retrieval system without the written permission of the author except in the case of brief quotations embodied in critical articles and reviews.

This book is a work of non-fiction. Unless otherwise noted, the author and the publisher make no explicit guarantees as to the accuracy of the information contained in this book and in some cases, names of people and places have been altered to protect their privacy.

WestBow Press books may be ordered through booksellers or by contacting:

WestBow Press
A Division of Thomas Nelson & Zondervan
1663 Liberty Drive
Bloomington, IN 47403
www.westbowpress.com
844-714-3454

Because of the dynamic nature of the Internet, any web addresses or links contained in this book may have changed since publication and may no longer be valid. The views expressed in this work are solely those of the author and do not necessarily reflect the views of the publisher, and the publisher hereby disclaims any responsibility for them.

Any people depicted in stock imagery provided by Getty Images are models, and such images are being used for illustrative purposes only.
Certain stock imagery © Getty Images.

Scripture quotations marked NKJV are taken from the New King James Version®. Copyright © 1982 by Thomas Nelson. Used by permission. All rights reserved.

Scripture quotations marked NIV are taken from The Holy Bible, New International Version®, NIV® Copyright © 1973, 1978, 1984, 2011 by Biblica, Inc.® Used by permission. All rights reserved worldwide.

ISBN: 979-8-3850-0026-5 (sc)
ISBN: 979-8-3850-0035-7 (e)

Library of Congress Control Number: 2023911048

Print information available on the last page.

WestBow Press rev. date: 9/28/2023

Do not remember the former things,
Nor consider the things of old.
Behold, I will do a new thing,
Now it shall spring forth;
Shall you not know it?
I will even make a road in the wilderness
And rivers in the desert.

Isaiah 43:18-19 NKJV

I would like to dedicate this book to my Lord and Savior Jesus Christ and to my two beautiful daughters, who I pray will always walk with God.

Also I would like to thank my mother Donna and my Aunt Mary Alice for proofreading the poems, my friend Abby for selecting the images for this book, and Westbow Press for making this book a reality.

Finally, to Preach and Pastor Ray, your friendship has been invaluable. Thank you for your Christian wisdom and guidance. This book would not have happened without you both in my life.

Table of Contents

Surrendering to God
Surrender 1
Give Him All 2

Following God
Follow Me 7
The Narrow Path 8

Choosing God
Are You Ready? 11
Two Roads But Only One to Take 12
The Choice 14

God's Sovereignty
Chance 17
Change 18
Not a Chance 19
God's Sovereignty and Our Freewill 20

The Goodness of God
The Man Named Jesus 23
My God: So Big and So Small 24
The Goodness of God 25
The Missing Piece 26

Heaven
Hold and See 29
Heaven 30
The Other Side 31
Homecoming: The Moment (In Honor of the Passing of My Nana, Marilyn Noll) 32

Reaching/Encouraging Others

An Encouraging Word 35
God Can Change Your Life (Cowritten With My Oldest Daughter) ... 36
A Moment 37

Purpose

The Importance of a Life 41
Purpose and Plan 42

Christmas: God Becomes Man

The Birth of Christ 45
Preparing the Way for the Lord (Zechariah and John the Baptist) 46
Joseph, Not Just a Carpenter 48
Mary, Favored by God 50
Prince of Peace 52

Being Thankful

Thankfulness 57

Grace

Beauty from Ashes 61
Faith and Works 62
East from West 63
The Gift 64
Unbound 65
Good Not Evil 66
Whose Child Are You? 67
A New Thing 69

Peace

The Peace of God 73
New Year's Eve 74

Time with God

Rest 77
Mary and Martha: A Lesson to Us Today 78
A Place 79

Christian Fellowship

Christian Friendship (Dedicated to Preach and Pastor Ray) 83

Love

The Greatest Is Love 87
The Blood 89

Surrendering to God

9/29/22

Surrender

To the world, surrender is not the way for something to end.
It's like you're giving up, losing a battle, allowing another to win.

It means you don't get your way or maybe lose control.
Most of time we want to be in charge, to say the yes or no.

But many times, as Christians, we are asked to do what the world sees as strange,
And surrender is an example where Christianity cuts against the grain.

For to truly be the Christian that Jesus wants us to be,
We must bow our knees, give all to Him, and surrender our destiny

To the One who holds the past, the present, and the future in His hand.
For He is the only One who can lead us to the promised land,

And surrender to Him is only the end of things better left behind,
Like sin, selfishness, living only for yourself, and the carnal mind.

But also surrender to Christ is the start of things that are so very sweet,
Like true joy, comfort, satisfaction, and—oh what wonderful—peace!

And in the end, we will get to spend forever in Heaven with our Lord,
So go against the tide. Let your desires die, and surrender to the One you were made for.

9/17/22
Give Him All

There once was a crowd full of men, women, boys, and girls.
They had come to hear the Master speak words that would change the world.

But the Master had compassion for the crowd and knew they needed to be fed.
"Where shall we buy bread for these people to eat?" to the disciples, the Master said.[1]

The disciples knew it would take so much money for all to have a bite.
They saw no way they could feed them all; there were so many in sight.

But a little boy was found with five loaves and two fish—possibly his lunch—
And he gave them to the Master. But how could so little feed so much?

But the Master took the fish and bread, blessed it, and gave it to His disciples to share,
And somehow they never ran out of food. There was enough for everyone there.

And after all were given what they needed, there remained twelve baskets full.
I can only think a basket for each disciple, as they needed to eat too.

So what's the moral of this story that happened so long ago?
That still today, in the Master's hands, He can multiply and make things grow.

---

[1] John 6:5 NIV.

So no matter how little you think you have to give the Lord above, Simply give it to Him—the great multiplier—and you will be amazed by what He does.

But there is also one final thing we can learn from that little boy that day. Give all to God, no matter how big or small, and God will make a way!

Following God

12/5/21
Follow Me

While walking by the Sea of Galilee, Jesus saw four men.
He asked them to stop catching fish and instead to follow Him.

And then one time, while walking by a tax collector's booth,
He told the man to follow Him, and then he had to choose

To get right up, not looking back, and to follow God.
As with man, He walked upon this earth; His precious feet did trod,

And all five men immediately left everything behind
And followed after Jesus when He said that it was time.

Matthew, Peter, his brother Andrew, James, and his brother John
Became a part of Christ's disciples—His plan all along.

But this same question Christ still asks, today, of me and you:
Will we also follow Him? It's up to us to choose.

So, reader, please heed today when you hear Christ's voice
Accept Him as your Lord and Savior if you haven't made this choice.

For then, you'll find true joy and peace. He'll never leave your side.
The greatest friend and comforter, with you He will abide.

11/16/21
The Narrow Path

The narrow path is the way
To get to that ever glorious day.

The path is straight and does not turn.
To keep on it, Godliness we must learn.

It veers not to the left or right
But runs straight into the everlasting light.

A choice I'm given, and I must make.
Is this narrow path the road I take?

And once I'm on, the choice is still
To stay the path through each valley, each hill,

To turn not to the left or right
But onward with the Spirit's might.

And at the end, the great city I will see
And the Jesus I love for eternity.

Choosing God

12/11/21
Are You Ready?

Are you ready to listen to God's voice today?
If Christ you've not accepted, will you come and be saved?

Are you ready to listen when God gives your path His light?
Will you walk in His beam, not turning left or right?

Are you ready to answer the question that may come even today?
When someone says, "Why Jesus?" what will you then say?

Are you ready if Christ comes in just five minutes' time?
Would you meet Him in the air, or would you be left behind?

So no matter where you find yourself on this very day,
If anything is in question, take it to God and pray.

For whatever your need is—His guidance or forgiveness of sin—
God will provide the answer if we just bring it to Him.

12/15/21
Two Roads But Only One to Take

In life there are many choices we all must make,
But really, there's only one of two roads that we can take.

Who will I marry? Will I have children? What job will I do?
Though important in the end, these decisions won't define you.

Should I go to college? Should I buy this or that place?
Won't matter so much at the end of your life's race.

For on a hill two thousand years ago, three men hung:
Two guilty sinners and the other, God's own Son.

One sinner remained defiant up until the end.
So close to God yet, without Him, eternity to spend

But the other one realized that he was lost
And called out to Christ to remember him from his cross.

In that moment, that man gained eternal life.
For Christ said, "Today you will be with me in paradise."[2]

So when you think of why there were three crosses on that day,
Don't think it was an accident that it turned out that way.

For the cross on one side represents the rejection of Christ,
But the cross on the other side, the acceptance of His sacrifice.

---

[2] Luke 23:43 NIV.

And on the cross in the middle hung perfect love,
So we, like the thief who cried out to Christ, can find Heaven above.

So there are really only two roads, but one you must take.
Choose wisely, for your decision will determine if Heaven you make.

9/27/22
The Choice

Throughout our lifetime, many a choice we will have to make.
Many are life changing, so carefully those we should take.

But even in a normal week, one thousand choices may come our way:
What to eat for every meal and if we take the time to pray.

Do we work hard on the job, make family time, watch the game on TV,
Plan to go to bed early, stay up late, or just decide to wait and see?

That some of life's choices are more important than others is clearly known,
For choosing a spouse has a far bigger impact than picking an Android or iPhone.

But one day, when we stand before God, only one choice will matter then:
If we want to enter Heaven for eternity with Him to spend.

And this choice echoes down through the ages, to every woman and man:
To accept or reject that God's Son completed salvation's plan

When He died on the cross and shed His perfect blood for you and for me.
For accepting or rejecting this sacrifice will, alone, determine where you spend eternity.

God's Sovereignty

11/17/21
Chance

What is chance?
A flip of a dime?

What is chance?
Something happening at just the right time?

But what if chance is something more?
What if chance was God moving pieces on His chess board?

What if what we think is only luck
Is God really getting us unstuck?

Putting people in our lives when it seems so right
Is God simply pulling us back to His light.

A better word than chance, I have a hunch,
Maybe that better word, actually, is God's providence.

11/28/21
Change

Change is all around, so much of it to see.
Just think back to when you were a kid with black and white TV.

A phone might have had a party line or rotary dial.
There were no flat screens, smart phones, or little emoji smiles.

Texting was unheard of unless you were writing a book.
Think back long enough and maybe there's no microwave to cook.

The internet was not around; a newspaper you had to find.
There was no such thing as Wi-Fi or possibly a landline.

And just think what lies ahead, what sights our grandkids will see.
It's hard to fathom what the future will bring with more technology.

But with one thing I'm certain, and with that I am sure:
My God, He will not be surprised, no matter what's in store.

For God is a constant, unchanging rock in the world that's a revolving door.
Praise God. "Jesus Christ is the same yesterday and today and" forevermore![3]

---

[3] Hebrews 13:8 NIV.

8/12/22
Not a Chance

There are times in life things just work out.
Or so it seems, and then we forget all about,

Like the time that car stopped without a moment to spare,
Or about to pass, you take a second look and see what had not been there.

Or the time you got a bigger promotion than you were even praying for
Instead of another you had wanted that had become a closed door.

Or the time when God gave you a friend going through a trial you once knew
So that you could help that person along and help them get through.

Or the time you met your true love and knew it at first sight
Because a buddy said, "Hey, would you like to go on a double date tonight?"

For you see, there are many things that seem to happen just by chance,
But many times we forget the One who really controls the dance.

So many things in this life we think are only happenstance
Have been His design from before even time and have nothing to do with chance!

10/10/22
God's Sovereignty and Our Freewill

God is God and knows all that is to come.
He knew all along He'd have to give His only Son.

God knew one thousand years ago that you would be born.
He also knew your name and every time your heart would be torn.

He knew your parents, your spouse, and how many children you would have,
For our God knows the future: all the good times and even the bad.

But in His sovereignty, God also allows us a choice
To turn away or listen when we hear His voice.

Now some would say a contradiction here they would find,
But I would have to disagree, for God lives outside of time.

And God asks us simply to believe, not to always understand,
For His ways aren't our ways and His wisdom so far above man's.

So if God says in Scripture that "whosoever will"
But also says, "For those God foreknew He also predestined," still[4]

The answer I know is that all of God's Word is true and will be kept,
Meaning Christ died for all and already knows who, in their freewill, His sacrifice will accept.

---

[4] Revelation 22:17 KJV; Romans 8:29 NIV.

The Goodness of God

11/18/21

The Man Named Jesus

There is a man who calms the sea,
Who watches over you and me.

He leads the way when the path is dim,
For He walks ahead, providing light for men.

If we turn to Him with all our hearts,
Call on His name, and from sin depart,

That name will be the one we call
When we reach His city, and at His feet we fall.

For this man is with me every day.
Every second, every minute, every hour, He leads my way.

For you see, this man is my best friend,
My Lord, my Savior, the beginning and the end.

For this man is more than just humankind.
He is Immanuel, God with us, truly divine.

1/7/22
My God: So Big and So Small

My God is so big; each star, He hung them all.
And my God is so small; He hears when we call.

My God is so big; He made each ocean and sea.
And my God is so small; He cares about you and me.

My God is so big; He put the mountains in their place.
And my God is so small; He cares for the trials we face.

My God is so big; He placed the planets around the sun.
And my God is small; He meets us daily, one on one.

My God is so big; He shaped each valley and hill.
And my God is so small; He always knows how we feel.

My God is so big; He beat death and rose from the dead.
And my God is so small; He knows each hair on our head.

My God is so big; He reigns in Heaven, on high.
And my God is so small; He knows each time that we cry.

My God is so big; He's eternal with no end and no start.
And my God is so small that He lives in my heart.

7/13/22
The Goodness of God

Look all around; it's for all to see—
The goodness of God for you and for me.

Look all around, for it's everywhere—
The signs of God's love, compassion, and care,

It's in the sunlight, falling to the ground,
And it's in the cry of a newborn baby's sound.

It's in the sky on a bright starry night
And in the hug of a mother before turning out the light.

It's in a dad playing catch with his son,
And it's in the flight of a young child's run.

It's in the joy of a bride walking down the aisle
And, even years later, when she looks at him and smiles

And says, "It's OK, dear. This is not the end.
Though I'm going away, I'll see you again."

For the goodness of God, one day we will see,
Is in Heaven, with Christ and loved ones, forever to be.

10/25/22
The Missing Piece

We are each made with an empty place in all our hearts,
Put there by the Creator right from the very start,

And in life, we try to fill it with oh so many things.
Some are even good, like a job, a family, or a wedding ring,

But many others are harmful that we hope will
Satisfy the emptiness inside that only One can fill.

And many turn to pleasures outside of God's plan,
But instead of filling the emptiness, it only becomes harder to stand.

For you see, this hole in our hearts was made by God above
When He formed you and me with His compassion and His love.

For there's only one thing that can fill the emptiness that's inside,
And that is Jesus Christ, who for you was crucified.

So if you are wandering through life and real satisfaction you seek,
You must put your trust in Jesus, for He, alone, is the missing piece.

Heaven

11/21/21
Hold and See

To hold His hand and see His face.
To stand in the presence of amazing grace.

To bow at His throne; to hold Him tight.
To be in the presence of perfect light.

To be able to look into His eyes with mine.
To know no more separation, eternity without time.

To walk hand-in-hand right by His side.
To touch the nail prints; to have nothing to hide.

To worship the King for eternity,

And to know Him without limit perfectly.
That, one day, is what Heaven means to me.

11/29/21
Heaven

Some of every tongue and tribe
Will be made, in Christ, alive

And will gather 'round His throne
To be called of Christ—His very own.

Walking on the streets of gold
Where no one will ever grow old,

Unknown peace, joy, and love
Will be felt in that land above,

And the best part of it all will be
Perfect union with Christ for eternity.

12/9/21
The Other Side

When we cross to the other side, sad we will not be,
For when we come to the other side, we'll find instant glory.

From on this side, death may seem like only a closed door,
But in reality, it's an opening to what God has in store.

No more troubles that we have now will happen again,
Instead perfect joy and peace and a love that will never end.

And, dear friend, just as real as the sun up in the sky
But even more real, the Son up there will never again die.

So when you think of loved ones who have made that journey yore,
If they knew Jesus, immediately they were with the Lord.

So listen, friend; trust Christ alone. It's something you must do,
So one day, when God says it's time, you will make that journey too.

1/12/22

Homecoming: The Moment (In Honor of the Passing of My Nana, Marilyn Noll)

There is a moment that I long to have that will be most precious and most dear.
A moment that will make each trial and pain in this life simply disappear.

A moment when I know that all is well, for all of eternity.
A moment when, in my arms, I hold everything that means so much to me.

A moment when I know that nothing bad can ever happen, not even once again.
A moment when I know I'm with the One who died for me, who is my greatest friend.

A moment when the feeling will be far more than anything I can currently describe.
A moment when I know never again will we have to say goodbye.

A moment when everything is made right and my joy and peace will be complete.
A moment that means never again will there be anything lacking to seek.

A moment when everything I've ever desired will be mine, and all is forever right.
And what is this moment? It's Heaven wrapped in the arms of Jesus, held tight.

Reaching/Encouraging Others

11/22/21
An Encouraging Word

Oh, the impact of the tongue—
So many different songs that can be sung.

A song of bitterness, rumor, and strife
Or a song of love and compassion like Christ's

Can change someone's day or even their life.
But will it salve like an ointment or cut like a knife?

So today, let us choose carefully what we say,
As it may be brought up on the great Judgment Day.

Let us choose to use words to heal and spread Christ
And back them up with action, as mere words won't suffice,

And together our words and actions will then be
A light shining for Christ for His eternal glory.

12/12/21

God Can Change Your Life (Cowritten With My Oldest Daughter)

You think every day; you think every hour.
How God has saved you with His wonderful power!

God has made you for a purpose and plan.
God has a job for every woman and man.

We need to all realize it's not just those who preach,
But we all serve Jesus full-time—our own circle to reach.

There are people you see who I'll never know.
God has placed them in your life—His love to show.

We all have an impact, a world that we touch.
Each day can make a difference for God's kingdom so much.

So whether you're a salesman, a nurse, or you teach,
You can reflect God's beauty in everyone you reach.

A kind work, a prayer, or telling someone your story
Can change someone's life and give God the glory!

So remember, no matter what profession you're in,
You go shine for Jesus, pointing others to Him.

2/2/22
A Moment

What is a moment? Just a quick flash of time?
But what is its impact? It depends on the kind.

For you see, most end and are remembered no more,
But some have a way of remaining far longer than we intended them for.

Maybe it was a harsh word in a moment of anger
Or a random act of kindness done to someone who's a stranger.

It could be an action meant to hurt one another
Or a kind, tender word to a sister or brother.

For in a moment, the destruction of many things have been born—
Kingdoms, relationships, marriages, and families apart have been torn.

But in other moments, something else has occurred.
Hope, joy, love, and healing are brought by an action or word.

So remember the power of each moment in time,
And with God always in control, His will, in word and action, you'll find.

Purpose

11/22/21
The Importance of a Life

What is the importance of a life?
To have a family, children, a wife?

To go to school to make big bucks?
To buy a fancy car or topped out-truck?

To become well-known or well-loved?
To rise in stature; to rise above?

So at the end you can look back and see,
How far you've come? How great is me!

I don't think that is what life is about;
Though, a loving family is very important, no doubt.

But all that matters in the end
Is to stand before my dearest friend

And hear these words coming from Him:
"Well Done, good and faithful servant!"[5] And then enter in.

---

[5] Matthew 25:21 NIV.

1/22/22
Purpose and Plan

You have a purpose, and God has a plan,
But there's something about these we must understand.

For when He made us, He had a purpose in mind,
For He made us each unique—one of a kind.

And the task that He's given each one of us to do
Can only be carried out exactly by me and by you.

So realize you're important, every woman and man,
For God made a miracle when He crafted us with His hand.

And with the help of this same hand, His purpose we fill fulfill,
One day hearing, "Well Done," when before Him we kneel.[6]

God's plan for us is not choosing what we want to do,
For if we follow our own hearts, everything we will lose.

No, God's plan is something much greater than that.
It's doing what He wants, and that's a matter of fact.

One thing brings God's plan and our purpose together,
And this is a choice we must make, for there is none better.

We must choose God's plan, not one of our making,
And God will honor us for this choice we are taking.

For the most important thing in this poem to understand
Is that to fulfill God's purpose, we must follow His plan.

---

[6] Matthew 25:21 NIV.

Christmas: God Becomes Man

11/26/21
The Birth of Christ

It's Christmastime, the best time of year,
A time to spend with ones held dear.

A time to shop for the latest toys
To put under the tree for girls and boys.

A time to watch snow fall to the ground.
A time to decorate with smiles all around.

A time to sing carols with family and friends.
A time for mistletoe, Christmas cards to send.

But if that is what Christmas is really about,
I'm afraid we've left the most important thing out.

For two thousand years ago, born in the hay,
Lay a little boy on Christmas day.

A baby who was yet a king,
Announced by herald angels sing,

Who came to live and then to die
So humans could have eternal life.

And that is the true meaning of Christmastime,
A babe in a manger sent to save mankind.

12/1/21

Preparing the Way for the Lord (Zechariah and John the Baptist)

There was an old man named Zechariah; a righteous priest was he,
Married to an old woman, Elizabeth. Forever childless she thought she would be.

But then one day in the temple, an angel appeared with great news
And told Zechariah, "Your wife Elizabeth will bear you a son," but he did not believe it was true.[7]

The angel Gabriel said, "You are to call him John ... and he will go on before ...
To make ready a people prepared for the Lord."[8]

Zechariah wondered how this could be with him and Elizabeth being so old,
And then he could not speak until the birth for not believing what he was told.

When he left the temple speechless, he could only gesture and nod,
And when he went home, his wife conceived, for nothing is impossible with God.

When Mary came to visit Elizabeth, her cousin, and walked through the door,
"Elizabeth was filled with the Holy Spirit" at the arrival of the mother of her Lord.[9]

---

[7] Luke 1:13 NIV.
[8] Luke 1:13, 17 NIV.
[9] Luke 1:41 NIV.

But also there was a reaction from a little, growing baby boy,
For the unborn child in Elizabeth also leapt inside her with great joy.

A few months later and the birth of Zechariah's son came,
But on the eighth day there was confusion about what should be his name.

So they gave Zechariah a writing tablet and asked what his son should be called,
And he wrote, "His name is John," and they marveled all.[10]

This was what the angel Gabriel said that the boy would be named,
And as soon as he wrote this, "his mouth was opened," and he would go on to proclaim,

That his son "will be called a prophet of the Most High" and "will go on before the Lord …
To give his people the knowledge of salvation through the forgiveness of their sins," what the Messiah would come for.[11]

For this child is John the Baptist, who prepared the very way for the Messiah that God would send:
The son of Mary, the Son of God, and our Savior—Jesus Christ, his very own cousin.

---

[10] Luke 1:63 NIV.
[11] Luke 1:64, 76–77 NIV.

12/17/21
Joseph, Not Just a Carpenter

Joseph was a simple young man; nothing special he appeared to be,
Betrothed to his young sweetheart, a teenage girl named Mary.

She became pregnant, and he must have thought, *How could this be?*
But being just and not wanting to cause shame, he chose to divorce her quietly.

But then Joseph had a dream where an angel did appear,
And the angel let Joseph know that there was nothing to fear.

The angel said, "What is conceived in her is from the Holy Spirit."[12]
What joy this must have brought to Joseph—these words—for him to hear it!

"You are to give him the name Jesus, because he will save his people from their sins."[13]
So Joseph awoke from his dream and, being righteous, obeyed what was said to him.

A census was then taken, and to his city went each man.
Being of the lineage of David, Joseph had to go to Bethlehem.

When they got into the city, Mary was nearly ready to deliver.
A warm place to have the child, she hoped the inn keeper could give her.

But they were turned away when they tried to stay at the inn,
And they quickly had to seek another place, as there was no room for them.

---

[12] Matthew 1:20 NIV.
[13] Matthew 1:21 NIV.

All they could find was a lowly stable in a city of what had to be strangers,
So alongside Joseph, she gave birth to her Son and laid Him in a manger.

But God was not through visiting Joseph; three more times He would guide him in dreams,
Directing him where to take his young family to protect them from Herod's schemes.

They went to Egypt and returned to an Israeli town called Nazareth when it was safe to be seen.
"So was fulfilled what was said through the prophets, that he would be called a Nazarene."[14]

But Joseph's job was just beginning; though, he'd already obeyed each dream,
For he had to raise God's Son. An impossible task it must have seemed.

But nothing is impossible with God if we trust and obey,
And though a simple carpenter, I believe he did this task in a remarkable way.

For though Scripture is silent about Joseph after Jesus's youth,
That he was chosen to be Jesus' earthly dad, this has to be the truth.

So when you think of Joseph, think of all God did with just a simple man,
For He took this young man—a carpenter—and used him in salvation's plan.

---

[14] Matthew 2:23 NIV.

12/18/21

Mary, Favored by God

Mary was a peasant girl, betrothed to a righteous man,
Not yet aware of the part she would play in God's master plan.

But suddenly this all would change when Gabriel did appear,
And oh, what amazing words did Mary unexpectedly hear.

Gabriel told Mary, "You have found favor with God. You will conceive and give birth to a son."[15]
Mary believed these words in her heart but wondered how it could be done,

So knowing no man, she asked the angel, "How will this be?"[16]
Gabriel said, "The Holy Spirit will come on you," meaning the Son of God she would conceive.[17]

And the angel told Mary that her cousin Elizabeth had become pregnant too. "For with God nothing will be impossible."[18] You see, there's nothing He can't do.

Then Mary said, "May your word to me be fulfilled," and the angel left.[19]
And Mary arose with haste and went to visit her cousin Elizabeth.

When Mary entered Elizabeth's house, her greeting was soon heard.
And Elizabeth's unborn baby leapt with joy, and she was filled with the Spirit upon hearing Mary's words.

---

[15] Luke 1:30–31 NIV.
[16] Luke 1:34 NIV.
[17] Luke 1:35 NIV.
[18] Luke 1:37 NKJV.
[19] Luke 1:38 NIV.

In time, there would be a census, and to Bethlehem she would go
Along with her husband, Joseph, who she had yet to intimately know.

And when they came to Bethlehem, she was ready to give birth
To the Savior of the world, who will bring humans peace on the earth.

So they went to the inn for a warm place to deliver their son,
But they were turned away, for there were no rooms. No, not even one.

So they found a lowly stable, and there amidst the hay
Was born the baby Jesus, and in a manager, He did lay.

Soon they would have company, as the shepherds would arrive,
Telling them of the wondrous angelic message they had just heard outside.

When Mary heard the shepherds tell of all they'd seen and heard,
She kept it all inside of her heart; so special were their words.

Eventually they took the baby Jesus to the temple, following the Law of Moses in their nation,
And righteous Simeon held baby Jesus in his arms and blessed God for letting him see His salvation.

And Mary would see her baby boy grow up to accomplish all God had Him to do,
For she was at the foot of the cross when Jesus died for her, for me, and for you.

So remember how God used a poor peasant girl to help bring about His salvation plan,
Giving birth to the hope of the entire world—Jesus—for every woman and man.

And as for Mary, her son would also become her Savior. For her sins, too, He did pay,
And inside her heart, He would always remain, as well, the little babe lying in the hay.

12/25/21
Prince of Peace

In a world that was torn with discord, war, sin, and strife
Came a little baby boy, born in a manger on Christmas night.

This baby was sent from on high, from Heaven above
And was the greatest gift of God's infinite love.

And though humankind had done their best to ravage the earth,
There was something different about this humble birth.

For God, in perfect wisdom, had a plan to restore His peace,
And in the stable, at Jesus's birth, God to earth did reach.

For this baby was unlike all others, not just an ordinary boy
But was both God and man, bringing the world great joy.

He shall be called the "Prince of Peace," the prophet Isaiah did say,
And the Prince of Peace came to earth on that Christmas day.[20]

"But wait," you say, "He went on to die, but the world remains unstill."
But the cross is key to God's master plan, and peace on earth will not come until

This Prince of Peace, who was born to die and rise up from the grave,
Comes back again a second time with all the saints He has saved.

And when He comes back this second time, He will make all things right,
And the completion of the God's plan will come, made possible that starry night.

---

[20] Isaiah 9:6 NIV.

For when Christ comes this second time, this turbulent earth He'll tame,
Destroying all forces of evil, and from Jerusalem, for one thousand years, He'll reign.

And during this millennial kingdom, this world will finally find perfect rest.
"The wolf will live with the lamb," for with the rule of the Prince of Peace, earth will be blest.[21]

But listen still; it's not done yet. For there will be a new Heaven and new earth,
And peace there will be for eternity. All because of that one humble birth!

---

[21] Isaiah 11:6 NIV.

Being Thankful

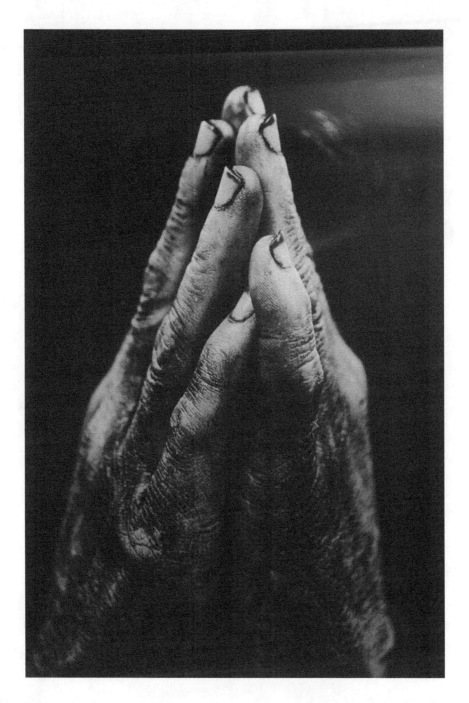

11/28/21

Thankfulness

As we live each day, how often we see
Something God made for you and for me:

A beautiful cloud, a rainbow, a tree,
A river, a stream, or even a sea.

A bird's flight in spring, colorful leaves in the fall—
The grandeur of creation, the majesty of it all.

But if we look a little deeper, something greater we'll see:
The crown of His creation—you and me!

For when Jesus came and died on the cross,
It was so humankind could be redeemed, not lost.

His love was so great for humanity.
He'd rather die than go without us eternally.

So when you see a sunset or a bird in the air,
Be thankful to God for His creation, His care.

But above all, let's thank God for His love of you and me—
A love on full display, shown in red at a place called Calvary.

Grace

11/30/21
Beauty from Ashes

It happens so often—a life torn apart
When sin wreaks its havoc; a fire it starts.

And when it is done with hurt all around,
All that appears left are ashes on the ground.

But then something amazing begins to unfold
As God looks down, and more than ashes, He beholds.

He reaches down gently and picks up the embers,
And kindly He reminds us it's not over. Remember!

There's a reason He came and died on the cross,
So ashes you won't remain for the wind to just toss.

No child, He came to die and shed His perfect blood,
So your ashes could be redeemed and made new with His love.

So, reader, please heed if sin has left you broken
And your life in ashes by misdeeds and words spoken.

Turn to Jesus Christ, and His pardon simply take.
And from a life full of ashes, something beautiful He will make.

For the past will be behind you, and the future that awaits
Will be a wondrous picture of God's amazing grace.

1/2/22
Faith and Works

"For it is by grace you have been saved, through faith," in Ephesians Paul did say,
Because on an old rugged cross, His only begotten Son the Father gave.[22]

And Jesus's brother James writes that "faith without works is dead,"
So some may see a contradiction in what they've just read.[23]

But the truth is there is no contradiction to be found here,
For the Bible makes the plan of salvation abundantly clear.

By faith and grace alone, we are saved to go to Heaven above.
It's a gift we can't earn but must receive, made possible by Christ's blood.

But this saving faith will also lead to a life that is totally rearranged,
For obedience to God will be the result, brought about by salvation's change.

So listen, friend, we are saved alone by faith and, into obedience, then are led,
For we aren't saved by faith and works but a faith that works, just like Luther said.

---

[22] Ephesians 2:8 NIV.
[23] James 2:20 NKJV.

1/9/22
East from West

I am so thankful that God does not give us what we deserve
Or repay us justly for the years that Him we have not served,

For His love is great, along with His compassion and His grace.
For on the old, rugged cross, Jesus Christ took our place,

And He removed every sin, forgiving them completely.
And as Micah wrote, "You will cast all our sins into the depths of the sea."[24]

Also God has the ability to do something that humans cannot,
For when He forgave me of all my sins, He also forgot.

And the Psalmist writes how wonderful, as Christians, we are blest,
For "He has removed our sins as far from us as the east is from the west."[25]

You may wonder why north and south is not used in this case
When describing how far our sin is removed by God's amazing grace.

I believe the answer is something that we now can plainly see,
For if you go north or south enough, together they will be.

But if you travel east or west, no matter how little or how much,
You will never meet the other, for there is no place they touch.

So remember, friend, how far from you God has removed your sin,
For they are in the sea of forgetfulness, never to be brought up again.

---

[24] Micah 7:19 NKJV.
[25] Psalm 103:12 NLT.

6/16/22
The Gift

The gift that was given so very long ago
Still, today, changes lives; this, for certain, I know.

For you see, this gift has changed even me
And took a life of sin and deceit and made it to be

A life of peace, joy, and hope with a future and a plan
That will fulfill the work God has, for me to do, guided by His hand.

And the reason I now walk redeemed, the Lord leading my way,
Being able, in His timing, to do all He has planned for me one day

Is that the gift that was given so many years ago in the hay
Came in that lowly stable but, in there, did not stay.

For after thirty-three years, the gift stretched His arms out on an old, rugged tree,
Spilling His perfect, holy blood for you and for me.

So even today, two thousand years later in time,
This gift transforms lives, for it has transformed mine.

8/17/22
Unbound

There was a time, not too long ago, I was held captive by my sin,
And there seemed no way of getting out and that it would have no end.

My heart and mind were both trapped in my own thoughts and desires.
Like the prodigal, I was down in the mud, the muck, and mire.

But I knew my life had to change, for peace I could not find,
So I turned to God, asked His forgiveness, for I knew that it was time.

And He reached down and picked me up, and I went from lost to found.
And with His grace, He broke my chains, and they fell to the ground.

So now I'm free to finally be what I was created for,
No longer in darkness bound by chains but unbound to serve the Lord.

3/9/22
Good Not Evil

What do you do when someone says an unkind word to you?
Forgive them, love them, and return words of mercy too.

What do you do when someone does you wrong?
Forgive them; love them; and with an act of kindness, respond.

What do you do when others talk behind your back?
Forgive them, love them, realize you've done it before, and cut them some slack.

What do you do when loved ones hurt you even more?
Forgive them, love them, and let the love of Christ restore.

For in the end, as Christians, we must chose
To return only good for evil, showing others Christ in you!

6/21/22
Whose Child Are You?

"Whose child are you?" someone may have asked
Many times throughout life to many a person in their past.

Whose child are you? A question many are glad to hear
But also a question that many more would fear.

"Whose child are you?" asked a man to a prince.
"I'm the child of the king," he answered without even a wince.

"Whose child are you?" asked another to a boy on the street.
"I don't know" was all he could muster, shuffling his feet.

"Whose child are you?" asked yet another to a woman once caught in sin.
But her answer surprised all who dared to listen in,

For she said, "I'm a child of not just a king but the greatest King of all."
And they laughed, and they jeered until she told them about His call,

How one night she awoke full of pain and despair.
Then she heard a voice gently whisper and knew He would not leave her there.

And she knew, from her past, who was calling her name,
And she cried out to God and was never the same.

So she told them, "Yes, I'm a child of the King
Through salvation in Christ, so now I can sing."

And the crowd went away, except one boy on the street.
He came slowly to the woman and said, "Your Father, let me meet."

So the woman showed the boy her true Father that day,
And he found the Lord on the street as he knelt down to pray.

And the next time the boy was asked, "Whose child are you?"
His answer wasn't "I don't know" but "He can be your Father too!"

9/23/22
A New Thing

In the book of Isaiah, God says, "See, I am doing a new thing!"[26]
It will be something amazing, something only He can bring.

"I am making a way in the wilderness," the Lord proclaims,
For there is nothing that our Savior cannot change.[27]

"And rivers in the desert," He also says will appear,
For God can bring life from death when He draws near.[28]

So if you are going through a trial that seems to never end
Or a hurdle that seems so high or a hurt that just won't mend,

Remember we serve a God who, in a moment, can turn things around
And make something new appear where there is only barren ground.

The key is to trust Him and surrender all to His loving will,
And God can make beauty out of our pain if before Him we kneel.

For our God knows the end from the start and sees what is to come,
And in His time, the desert will flow with rivers of relief from the Son.

---

[26] Isaiah 43:19 NIV.
[27] Ibid.
[28] Isaiah 43:19 NKJV

Peace

12/4/21
The Peace of God

The peace of God, it calmed the sea.
The peace of God calms you and me.

The peace of God, it does so much.
The peace of God from the Master's touch.

The peace of God can change a life.
The peace of God guides us through the night.

The peace of God circumstance can't change.
The peace of God, it will remain.

The peace of God, its value who can find?
The peace of God worth more than treasure of any kind.

The peace of God comes from Heaven above.
The peace of God made possible by Christ's love.

The peace of God a sinner will gain.
The peace of God when he calls on Jesus's name.

The peace of God and asks forgiveness for his sins.
The peace of God and, in a moment, is born again.

And the peace of God passes all understanding
Not found in this world, for it's only something God can bring.

12/31/21

New Year's Eve

The final hours are winding down on another year,
And I can sit and think about all my concerns and fears.

But the truth is that the Master commands us not to worry,
For we don't really need to sit and fret or be in a hurry.

For no matter how much humankind tries to think and make their plans,
The future is held securely by the One with nail-scarred hands.

So our task is to follow God and stay inside His will
And know that He alone is God and, as the Psalmist says, "Be still."[29]

For if the One who holds the future is the captain of our ship,
He will guide us safely in the new year, regardless of the waves that hit.

For two thousand years ago, He calmed the sea with just a simple command.
"Peace, be still!" and the winds died down at the words of the God-man.[30]

So next year, when life's trials come and too heavy is your load,
Listen to the Psalmist again. Be still, and know who's in control.

For the same command Jesus gave that day, on the Sea of Galilee,
Will still work for us if we trust in Him, for He'll also calm our sea.

---

[29] Psalm 46:10 NIV.
[30] Mark 4:39 NKJV.

Time with God

12/19/21

Rest

We live in a world of constant change, moving to and fro.
It seems we're always on the run with somewhere else to go.

We tend to worry and to fret about what each day brings
And get so busy we forget about the important things.

So let me tell you a secret; one you may already know.
In this race we call life, we'd better take it slow

And set aside our daily list and find a quiet place.
Spend time in prayer and the Word, and earnestly seek God's face.

In this time with God, you will find rest for your soul when it is weary,
And your day will change, brightening what had seemed so dreary.

So listen, friend; if you think you don't have time to read and pray,
The truth is you're really too busy not to spend time with Him each day.

For when you meet with Jesus and you do what's right,
Your daily load will lessen, for as Christ said, "My yoke is easy and my burden is light."[31]

---

[31] Matthew 11:30 NIV.

12/27/21

Mary and Martha: A Lesson to Us Today

Jesus journeyed to Bethany and came to a house there one day—
A home with two Godly sisters—and He was welcomed to stay.

And what each chose to do that day is a lesson for you and me,
For one sister was named Martha and the other sister, Mary.

Martha was so busy running around and serving all of her guests
That she became very annoyed when her sister, Mary, decided to rest

At the feet of the Lord, Jesus Himself, listening to each word intently.
So Martha, working alone, told Jesus, "Tell her to help me!"[32]

But Jesus then told Martha an important truth in no uncertain terms:
"Mary has chosen what is better, and it will not be taken away from her."[33]

So when life has you busy in every direction and always on the run,
Always remember to stop each day and spend time with the Son.

And a treasure of peace and joy each day with Jesus you will find,
For the God of the universe has a meeting with you if you just have the time!

---

[32] Luke 10:40 NIV.
[33] Luke 10:42 NIV.

6/17/22
A Place

There is a place where I can go; a place where I can hide;
A place of comfort, rest, and peace; a place I can abide;

A place where I can lay my worries, doubts, and all my fears;
A place where I can take my troubles, for I know that He will hear;

A place where I can simply be what I was created for;
A place where I can talk and listen to the One who never shuts the door.

For in this place, the longings of my heart and fulfillment finally meet.
Where is this place of perfect rest? It's found at Jesus's feet.

Christian Fellowship

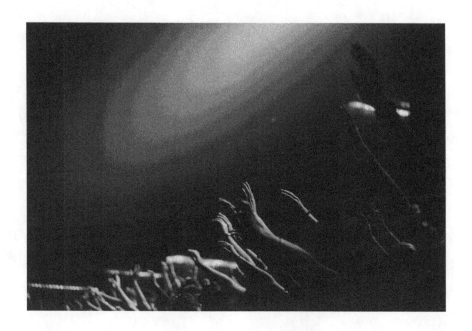

12/23/21
Christian Friendship (Dedicated to Preach and Pastor Ray)

A true Christian friend, if you find, is a wonderful treasure indeed,
For true Christian friendship is something every one of us needs.

A true Christian friend will be someone who will be there at all times
And know when they need to be firm and when they need to be kind.

But a true Christian friend will also be willing to tell you the truth
Even if it's hard for you to hear, for they want the best for you.

They will encourage you, and along life's way, your burdens they will help bear.
They will be a listening ear, but also listen to them, for Godly wisdom they will share.

They will hold you accountable, keeping you strong as you grow in the faith.
They will walk beside you, showing Christ's love all along life's race.

For "a cord of three strands is not quickly broken," the Bible does proclaim.[34]
And who is this third strand in Christian friendship? Jesus is His name!

---

[34] Ecclesiastes 4:12 NIV.

Love

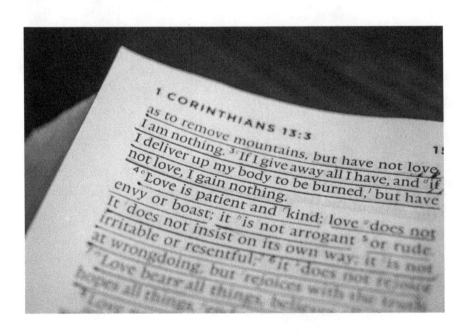

10/28/22

The Greatest Is Love

In I Corinthians 13, Paul writes, "Now these three remain:
Faith, hope, and love."[35] Three characteristics of a life changed.

And Paul also writes that one of these is above them all:
"The greatest of these is love," for it stands the most tall.[36]

"But why," you may ask, "is love what is supreme?
For in the life of a Christian, all three are needed, it would seem."

So I'll give you some ideas why I think love is on top,
For God's love is eternal and will never stop.

See, before there was time and need for hope or faith,
The Triune God existed and, within this, love had an integral place.

So love was the first of these three that was to ascend,
For it had no start and, within the Godhead, had always been.

Now don't get me wrong; faith and hope are so vital as well,
For by faith in God's grace, we are saved to Heaven from Hell.

And what a hope that brings to a Christian every single day,
Knowing that all of our sins are forgiven, completely wiped away.

But the reason that faith saves and we have hope for Heaven above
Is only made possible by the ultimate act of God's great love.

---

[35] 1 Corinthians 13:13 NIV.
[36] Ibid.

For on the cross, the Father sent His Son for our sins to bear.
Oh, what love of the Father and Son that held Him up there.

And one day in Heaven, faith and hope will be no more,
For our faith will be sight, having all we have ever hoped for.

But in that blessed place, love will still abide
And will never end on that glorious other side.

"So why is love the greatest of all?" one may ask again.
For it's what held Christ on the cross - having no start and no end.

12/12/22
The Blood

The entry to Heaven came at highest cost,
For it was purchased by a Lamb stretched out on a cross.

And this Lamb was without blemish, having done no wrong,
Completely innocent and full of love, hanging where we belonged.

And the truth is He gave His life freely to us that day,
So a path could be made to Heaven, for there's only one way.

And this path is the same for all, made possible by Christ's love,
For the entry to Heaven never changes and is always the blood.

Printed in the USA
CPSIA information can be obtained
at www.ICGtesting.com
LVHW091153140624
783126LV00012B/29